The Essence of Wisdom and Life

Praise for The Essence of Wisdom and Life

"Through poetry and prose, Dahveed invites the reader to contemplate the human experience. He shares his life lessons in concise, but deeply felt lines of lyrics pushing us to examine our own lives and the legacy we leave behind. It is clear that Dahveed has not merely existed, but has experienced life and taken the time to reflect on its journey. He does not shy away from expressing personal convictions or creeds and commits to sharing his insights into the world as it is, and as it should be. His thoughtful and bold soul appears clearly in the pages of words and photographs which beckon you to the next corner of discovery. "

- Jennifer Lynn Head

"Certainly, writing is what Dahveed was meant to do. His poetic words provide inspiration and healing; offering a soothing voice during difficult times and grounding us in thinking about a greater purpose in life. His writing creates a space for daily reflection that has easily replaced my once-a-day meditation book. *The Essence of Wisdom and Life* will lure you to read it again and again---for introspection, and to hear Dahveed's thoughtful reflections from a newfound perspective."   - Erika M Hess, M. S.

"A truly amazing piece, one that will make you take a retrospective look at how you approach your friendships, love and life. It's a good reminder of how to approach life in a more open minded and optimistic way. Dahveed demonstrates through poetry how hopefulness and forgiveness can help with our own healing."

- Lesli Mathis, LCSW

"Once again Dahveed has mastered the art of poetry. The Essence of Wisdom and Life reveals one's inner thoughts, passion, and reflection on life. This book really spoke to me and allowed me to search deep within and recognize the true person that I am. I recommend anyone who needs soul searching to read this book as it is truly a keepsake to benefit from and enjoy." - **Shana Ayscue, President/CEO, STA Technologies, LLC**

Author's Note

I have intentionally omitted a table of content. You, the reader are about to embark on a continuous flow of words through a poetic journey. Within the pages of this book, I have provided you with prompts so that you can take assessment of who you are and the journey you are on. Feel free to share your responses with me by sending me either an email or a letter to the address provided on the copyright page. In saying this . . .

There comes a time in each of our lives where we go through a period of transition. Our minds are sharper, we see life a little clearer than before, and we begin to question our life's path; the final journey. When this happens, we must take full advantage during this period of time; it may be awhile before it comes along again. Take stock of your current situation, your journey, and ask yourself; is this where you want to be. Are you walking the right path? Now is the time to make the necessary changes to continue on your life's journey. Let your journey begin in your search for The Essence of Wisdom and Life.

Changes I need to make for my life's journey:

The Essence

of

Wisdom and Life

Dahveed

Dahveed's Voice and Vision

The Essence of Wisdom and Life

First Printing, December 2011

Copyright ©2011 Dahveed aka D. A. Isley All Rights Reserved

ISBN-13: 978-0615575971

ISBN-10: 0615575978

BISAC: Self-Help / Personal Growth / General / Poetry

Cover design and interior photography by Dahveed

Edited by: Heather Mann, Ph.D.

Book title suggested by: Juree Serene

Published by Dahveed's Voice and Vision

Web Page: http://www.dahveed.com

Email: dvv@dahveed.com or dahveedwrites@gmail.com

No part of this book may be reproduced, stored in a retrieval system, or transmitted, in any form, or by any means (electronic, mechanical, photocopying, recording, or otherwise) without prior written permission from the author. Any members of educational institutions wishing to photocopy part or all of the work for work in an anthology, should send their inquiries to Dahveed's Voice and Vision, P. O. Box 28764, San Diego, California 92198.

For

WISDOM ~ LAVERNE GOINS

Teachers are a child's first introduction into the world of knowledge and understanding the essence of wisdom and life. It is now that I understand why you pushed me so hard. You saw something in me that I was not ready to see. You taught me as you taught your own children; in turn, we teach our children and assist them on their life's journey.

FOREWORD

This is a remarkable compilation of inspirational poems, stories and photographic art that depict various moments of realization in life. Author, Dahveed supplies the reader with a variety of wonderful ideals to live by. These ideals serve as reminders about the benefits of making positive changes in our lives and the positive impacts that we can have on the lives of others.

The story retreats to an eloquent depiction of the very beginning of the formation of the world and of the universe to remind us and to shed light on the many magical processes responsible for who we are, and why we are.

Dahveed utilizes vivid imagery, meaningful themes and raw emotion to challenge people into the realization that they can grow, change and be who they want to be. This book is truly touching and it contains innumerable thought provoking and conversation provoking concepts. Dahveed allows people to witness the world with freedom from conventional forms of conceptual constraint.

He encourages readers to appreciate the little things in life. Readers are also inspired to actively seek and choose their destiny. The author engages the reader to literally contribute to the text by evaluating and writing their own prompted reflections into his book. It takes the reader on a therapeutic journey toward empowerment and self-discovery.

This is the kind of book that you not only want to read but you will feel the need to own and refer back to it regularly.

- Stephanie L. M. Abel, M.A.

PROLOGUE

It was in two thousand and ten when I took a seat at the park, not quite dark, listening to the birds go "tweet, tweet, tweet" while a wintry breeze briskly grazed across my face as I stared up to the heavens, asking myself - "why do we judge others by the color of their skin when souls are colorless?"

I pulled out my pen and wrinkled pad, carefully chose the words that would spill dark, the ink of nothingness onto a blank sheet of lined paper that was once used for birds to sing their lullabies as the sun slowly dimed its rays, attempting to make its way through the thickness of the leaves that fell upon the ground on which I now choose to walk a different path on this day while taking my seat upon a bench that did not recognize color and began to reminisce of those days gone by, when my name was nothing more than "boy" until I became a "man" and realized that I was born equal; not first, second, third, above, or beneath others that came before or after me as I envisioned the world from the beginning when it was all dark, no breeze, no birds singing their sweet lullabies, no trees swaying in the wind, or rain falling to bring new life onto a planet in which we now call home. Before time there was no color. Before time there was no hatred. Before time there was no one separating us into a class of people that would one day turn on their own . . . people, turn on their own children as I flip the page to begin a new chapter, a new paragraph, a new beginning – an understanding of what this is that we call "life"; as the crescent shaped moon fills the night, surrounding itself with the twinkling of stars that many wish upon in hopes for a better tomorrow; and so I remember; I cry, I laugh, I smile, as my heart fills with joy that . . . children don't see color.

We tend to forget that children are impressionable, a carbon copy, a reflection, a micro-recorder, a video recorder, as they say what they hear and do what they see; being the mirror image of those that created them, surrounded them, and not taking into consideration that one day that child may take a journey down the wrong path, the right path if we equip them with the tools that will help them to succeed on their journey which will be different than the one we took as they discover that our life was filled with hate, mistrust, and the misunderstanding of people, nations which brought about wars making widows and widowers, fatherless and motherless children; leaving hundreds of thousands and millions laying in cold dirt wondering what did we do wrong, go wrong as a people and can our children fix the mess that we created – oh, what a burden to place upon those that we created, the mess we created, because we became selfish, the richest of all nations allowing greed to take control, take over as we spent our children's inheritance that they will not be able to use for their own children if they are unable to fix the mess that we created – CORRECTION, those that were elected to lead us down the right path, led us down the wrong path into an economical downfall leaving millions jobless; occupying Wall Street, occupying Atlanta to Philadelphia, occupying California to Alaska, occupying . . . my thoughts as I use my voice, my pen, to write my words, my vision across the pages of your mind as I continue my search for . . .

The Essence of Wisdom and Life

In order to get to the end, you must start at the beginning.

In The Beginning . . .

Darkness enveloped the universe with nothingness; a void that needed to be filled. Slowly, effortlessly, the darkness began to dissipate and could no longer stay as dim as it once had before. Far off in the great distance a flickering light appeared that grew and grew until all that was dark became bright and clear. Light itself began to fade and could no longer illuminate what was once dark. Darkness fell upon the universe once more. Then, there was light. Then there was life.

Like a whisper, two lips forming to blow atmospheric gases throughout what was once dark to cause a chain reaction that formed celestial bodies of mass orbiting what was once filled with nothingness. The sphere shaped bodies of mass were as empty as what was once darkness. Like marbles bumping into one another dropping seed-like particles from its outer shell, they dispersed and became as distant as the dark from the light. As the particles fell onto each celestial mass, the light illuminated them and organisms began to form. Then there was life.

Darkness fell over all that was formed once again and when light shined on all the organisms that had been created; there was still silence, still nothing. Coldness began to cover what was again a void, and a streak of electrical current filled the darkness. As if a thousand hands clapped in unison, a loud thunderous noise shook the orbiting mass as a thick layer of moisture surrounded and enveloped it with a liquid substance that caused all to regenerate. Light reawakened to brighten all that was dark. Then there was life.

Dust . . . blew as though trying to speak. Forming, breaking down - once again, forming to recreate itself into . . . what began to move across the surface of this newly created mass that took its place in what was once darkness, emptiness.

Then there was . . .

LIFE

When we enter the world, our hair is thin, we are wrinkled, and we cry because we are scared and uncertain if we want to be here or not. If we've lived a full life - when we die our hair has thinned, we are wrinkled, and we cry because we don't want to leave.

I am Buddhist

I am Christian

I am Hindu

I am Jewish

I am Muslim

I am African American

I am Asian

I am Caucasian

I am Hispanic

I am Indian

I am fat

I am skinny

I am short

I am tall

I am young

I am old

I am an enigma . . .

I am The Essence of Wisdom and Life

The Key of Life

The key to understanding life is finding out which doors to open, which ones to close at the right moment and accepting the reality of YOUR choice.

A One-Time Offer

Above all, live your life one day at a time. Don't be in a rush to make tomorrow come any sooner than it needs to get here. What's important in YOUR life at this moment, at this very second . . . is YOU. Your main objectives to consider should be –

What makes me happy

What makes me want to be successful

What goals do I want to accomplish for myself

How much time do I want to give myself to accomplish these goals

As young adults, you are too much in a hurry to get married, settle down, and have children - that time will come in its OWN TIME. But for now, everything should be about YOU. Take some time and explore all of your options before making any decisions that YOU may regret later in life. Your life is a ONE TIME offer - so make every moment count with no regrets later. Learn to accept your mistakes, and look at them as a lesson learned. This is YOUR moment in life to make everything count. YOU are in charge of your destiny – don't force it, let it happen.

What makes me happy?

What makes me want to be successful?

What goals do I want to accomplish for myself?

How much time do I want to give myself to accomplish these goals?

Nothing to Something

It's a beautiful thing when you come from "nothing" to "something" and can understand through life that it wasn't all for "nothing" while enjoying the fruits of your labor as you live your dreams.

Crossroads of Life

Throughout the crossroads in life, people often find themselves looking back to what brought them to a certain place and time. They sit, think, reflect and realize that the choices they made were not choices at all; but rather a grand design. The design allows us to see what would, could, and did happen to bring us to this point and time.

What choices did I make when I came to a crossroad in my life?

A Child's Path

A child's path is directed by how they are led not by who they follow. Teach them to become leaders, not followers; and in turn they will share their knowledge.

As a child reaches out, grab hold and don't let go . . . they will thank you for it tomorrow.

Children often see things that adults take for granted. Take a step back and see through their eyes.

How you respond to a child today makes a difference in how they will respond tomorrow.

Ways in which I can make a difference in a child's life:

Even the smallest voice can awaken an entire nation.

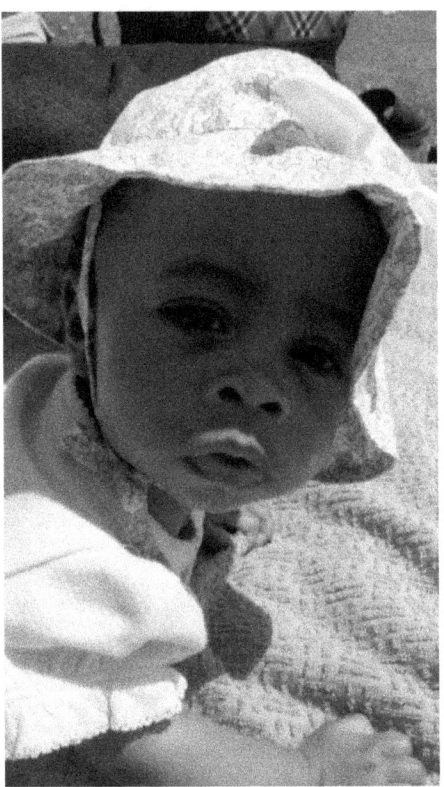

Miscommunication

A parent was teaching their child the difference between hot and cold. The parent was steaming some rice and the steam came up into the air. The parent looks at the child and says "hot." The little child looks at the parent and repeats "hot." "Yes", says the parent, "hot." Again, the little child repeats, "hot." A few days later, the parent is holding the little child and opens the freezer door. The little child sees the cold steam and says "hot." The parent looks at the child and says, "no, cold. This is cold." The child looks at the parent confused and says "hot." The parent then repeats and says, "No, this is cold." Frustrated and confused, the child closes the freezer door on the parents hand and says, "Ouch."

Ways to build on my communication skills:

An Open Mind

An open-mind is one that does not judge or criticize; but looks at each situation as a learning tool to enhance his or her own mind.

Lasting Thoughts

As the years pass us by, we often overlook or forget those that brought a smile on our faces, something to laugh at, or a thought to ponder. We later look back on their life, our life, and say to our-selves; "I wish I had kept in touch." It's a blessing when one leaves us with such a thought.

I need to reconnect with:

We as humans often judge, assume, and speculate how one is as an individual. If we only take the time to read the book until the final chapter, the last page; we will then get a clear understanding of the message that is being disseminated. All of us must be and will be accountable of how we view others. Everything nor everyone is not always as it seems. We need to look more on the inside before judging the outside.

I have misjudged or misunderstood:

Every day is different than the next. We have our bad days and good days; but the beauty of the two, we have a chance to make the necessary changes if our faith and belief is strong enough to hold true to what is in our hearts.

What's the point of growing flowers if the rain doesn't come to quench the thirst of the seeds that lay beneath the dirt as the roots from the grass peek out to get a glimpse of the sun that is shaded by the clouds waiting to shed its tears?

A Priceless Journey

A young man was walking down the street and sees an object shinning in his path. He walks up to it and says "oh, just a penny." He keeps walking. Two minutes later, a homeless man carrying all that he owns in a bag, walks the same path, sees the penny, picks it up, and puts it in his pocket. The young man continues on his journey and sees another shinny object. He walks up to it and says "oh, just a nickel." He keeps walking. The homeless man comes by and sees the nickel. He picks it up and puts it in his pocket with the penny. The young man continues his journey and sees two quarters, a dime, a nickel, and a penny in his path. He stops, stares at it for a second and then keeps walking. The homeless man comes by, sees the loose change, picks it up and again, puts the change in his pocket.

Twenty minutes go by and the homeless man arrives at his destination. He walks into the store to purchase a cup of coffee. He walks up to the cashier who had just arrived to start his shift and gives him the loose change. The cashier says it is not enough money. He then takes a second look at the change and screams out "Oh my goodness!" The homeless man was startled and asked "what is it?" The young man explains that the coins he had given him were collectibles, worth more than a few hundred dollars. "Where did you get these?" the young man asked. The homeless man told him that he saw another man walk pass the coins and kept going, so he picked them up.

Often when you overlook the smaller things in life, the bigger rewards will pass you by.

Some of the smaller things in life I have overlooked or taken for granted:

Defining Your Future

Often, people allow the past to dictate their fate; their future. They refuse to move forward and remain stagnant in a world they believe owes them everything because of the rotten luck they had. Then there are those who have had the worst luck growing up; abandoned, abused, and they take what happened to them and use it as a stepping stone to catapult their future. In this instance; their past is what allowed them to be who they have become; an advocate, a teacher, a speaker. They turned their negative into a positive. Sometimes in life; in order for us to move forward, we need to take a step back and see what bought us to where we are. But we need to do this in a way that will not allow us to be caught up in that "bad" space where we should not be - in the past.

If we forget about today, what's the use of looking forward to tomorrow? Our past often defines our future.

How has my past defined my future?

Forgiveness

One of the hardest things in life to do is to forgive. In order for us to forgive others, we must look deep within our own souls and search for what we need others to forgive us for. Only then one realizes that forgiveness comes from within, not from just our words.

What do I need others to forgive me for?

Who do I need to forgive and what do I need to forgive them for?

Why has it taken me so long to forgive someone?

When speaking out of anger; remember that our words are like a goose-down comforter that's full of feathers; once we wear it out and the feathers burst from the seams, they are hard to get back.

Words I need to take back that I have said to someone out of anger:

Ways in which I control my anger towards someone:

The beauty of growing older is acknowledging that everything you've learned, everything you've accomplished was for a reason. And if you've taken all that the world has provided for you and used it to your advantage; then you have fulfilled your life's purpose.

Ones path in life can travel down many roads, through many valleys, curves and hills. When the road one chooses leads to success and acknowledgment of that journey, it is then that they have found one's own true self, their own life's journey, their purpose.

I believe that my purpose in life is:

The Answer

Look

Beyond today,

Open your mind to tomorrow.

Look

Beyond hate,

Find peace where there's none.

Look

Beyond YOU,

Realize there's more.

Look

Beyond life,

Search for the meaning.

Look

Beyond prayer . . .

The answer

The Color of Life

Red,

White,

Yellow,

Pink . . .

A rose is only a rose until you smell the beauty that expels from the petals leaving you with the beauty of life.

Knowing When To Slow Down

A Rabbi and his student were walking to synagogue. The student notices a mass of people going in the same direction. The student says to the Rabbi; "Rabbi, I know a much faster way to synagogue around all of these people." The Rabbi kept on the same path, while the student chose a different one, a faster one.

An hour goes by and the student arrives at the synagogue, but does not see the Rabbi waiting outside for him. He walks in and hears the Rabbi saying the *Berakhah* for *Kiddush*. After shul, the student approaches the Rabbi and asks; "Rabbi, I walked a different path that would get me to synagogue faster, but when I arrived, you were saying the *Berakhah* for *Kiddush*. How did you get here before me?" The Rabbi smiled at the student and replied "Throughout our lives, we find ourselves rushing as time passes us by; and through all the confusion, we've accomplished very little. Sometimes we need to slow down and take a step back in order for us to move forward. It is only then that we can see the journey that lies before us.

I need to slow down so that I can:

Touching one life can make the difference between failing and succeeding.

I have made a difference in the lives of these individuals:

Validation

When we search for "ourselves" in the eyes of others, we have imprisoned our own-selves in believing that our self-worth is nothing unless others validate who we are. Unless we approve of whom we are, what we are, and what we are capable of doing as an individual, only then we will have released "ourselves" from our own imprisonment. We are in charge of our own life's destiny and what we do and become can only be validated by our accomplishments and failures; not by what others may think of us.

In what ways do I validate who I am as an individual?

We remember what we want to remember and forget those things that we choose to forget. Eventually, what we choose to forget comes back to remind us of who we once were and what we once did. Remembering who we are allows us to accept the changes and challenges in our lives so that we can live to make tomorrow a better tomorrow.

The things or circumstances that helped me remember where I came from:

When we are hurt and shed our tears, we are cleaning our hearts so that we can move forward and start anew. Yet, the pain still remains so that we can remember what it took for us to reach the end of our journey.

How has shedding my tears allowed me to move forward with my life?

Why do we judge people by race, religion, and social status? We are all as individual as the fingers on our hands. Like our fingers, it often takes more than one to accomplish a task.

I have assumed the worse about someone and later regretted it. I assumed that:

Often we are blinded by things that we do not wish to see or acknowledge. It sometimes takes someone else to allow us to see through their eyes before we can get a clearer view.

Knowledge is the key that can open almost any door once you know how to unlock it.

Through knowledge, I have opened the following doors by using the correct key of life:

Directionally Challenged

Left, right, up and down . . . the view is never the same. Only when you look in one direction, your options become limited. Choose your path wisely.

Faith

Seeing the impossible through the eyes of an unbeliever and acknowledging that is not what one thinks of life; it's how you live it.

How has my faith changed my life?

Impressions

Money, fame, wealth does not impress everyone. Those things come and go. What often does make an impression upon someone is what one does for others out of the kindness of their heart. That's when you leave an everlasting footprint on one's soul.

What impresses me about someone?

Healing

The act of taking care of one's inner-self before you can move forward and continue your journey.

The things I do to take care of ME:

THE ESSENCE OF . . .

The Essence of Me

Who I am . . .

Not desiring to be who or what you are as my life progresses to new levels of knowledge and insights into the world that surrounds my very existence because I chose to be ME and walked a different path than you, him, or her while overcoming obstacles that would slow my motion while rebuilding my faith and not allowing for a complete halt; but a momentary lapse of reflection that led who I am to become ME.

The Essence of You

You are . . .

The very being that crossed oceans, rivers, streams, and walked through deserts that cooked sand, jungles that came alive at night, streets that never sleep; to make it to your destination of dreams that your father or mother never fulfilled but instilled in YOU the power, courage, the fortitude to be more than what him, her, or they said that YOU could not be because YOU were not them; instead YOU defied all the critics and remained true to being just YOU.

I see myself as:

The Essence of Marriage

Marriage is a journey of caring, communicating, forgiving, and loving each other as if the two of you are the only ones left in the world. We often care about that person's needs and desires and put their needs above our own. We communicate what we feel, how we feel, and express those feelings in many different ways. When things are at a disagreement, we find it within ourselves to ask for forgiveness; only then, we find harmony. As long as your love for one another is strong, you can find that no matter what obstacles come before you, you can overcome them. Throughout the years, marriages for the most part endured a lot and have found ways to overcome the trials and tribulations of life. This is mostly done because as humans, we often put love first. Love for another person is very powerful. No matter what; love can often withstand the journey of life.

What journey do I want my marriage to take?

The Act of Love

Making love is not just a sexual act...

If you don't use your head and heart, you're only going through the motions, with no emotions.

The Essence of Death

It is what it is, this thing that we call death as we are designed to take our first breath that will only lead to our last breath that reaches out to grab hold of what is to become a final journey into the unknown as the soul releases and grasps hold of the last shimmer of what was once its house that surrounded and protected it from all harm but not the pain that it suffered while being housed, not the love that it enjoyed while being housed, not the thoughts that manifested itself in the rented space that is now vacated, emptied, abandoned – lifeless, as all of the lights have gone out and never to be turned back on again as the coldness sets in and stiffens the foundation that once moved, danced, and travelled to other unknown places except the one place that it was not allowed to travel because it still had life that occupied a house where the rent is no longer due, overdue and will not be renewed; contract cancelled out, no bargaining with the landlord in hopes to renew for one more year; even one more month would make things a little better, make changes to undo what can't be undone as the paper is now stamped . . . "expired lease" with no options to buy out a contract that had no warnings, no guarantees, no final balloon payment, and an end date that was uncertain as the house is now cleaned; moved into its new location beside others that will slowly wither away into the dust from which it came; as those we knew stood above, looking down in tears of sadness, happiness to realize that you have reached a level that they have not yet achieved, but will; as they continue on their life's journey in hopes to move into a location next to you.

This is how I want to be remembered:

Inevitably, the actions we choose may one day affect someone else's life. Prepare yourself for the consequences of those actions.

Truth or Consequences

Bold-faced

Broken promises

Compulsive

Deception

Exaggeration

Fabrication

Plagiarism

White – with each lie, you need another lie to replace the first lie in order to cover the real truth about the lie you told in the first place. Regardless of what may have happened, it is easier to tell the truth, face the consequence, and learn from that experience.

The lies I've told that I had to pay a consequence for:

Dream a little dream and watch how BIG it can get once you put it into action.

My little dream is:

My BIG dream is:

When seeking counsel, listen whole heartedly to the person that is speaking to you. They did not seek you out; it was you that sought after their wisdom. Once you have received that knowledge, it is up to you to act upon it. As it was given to you, you too must share it with others.

When giving of yourself to others, charity, do not boast; it makes the gift worthless. Greater are the rewards if your gift is made in private.

What have you given to someone that no else knows about except you and the receiver of the gift?

Even as an apple falls from a tree, it rots and withers away.

You too shall be hurt; but you can heal.

Speak from your heart the words that form from within your soul. If you deny yourself your own truth, what good does it do for someone seeking the wisdom you have to offer?

A Little Old Story

A young family was invited to their friends house for an evening gathering. They had taken their eleven month old child with them During the evening as people were arriving, they would see the little child and compliment how adorable the child was. Some of the people even walked up, tried to touch the child; but the child hugged on to her daddy and wouldn't let go. Then there were some that ignored the child as if the child was not there at all. This kept occurring during the course of the evening.

Everyone was talking, eating, and having a good time. The little child sat on the floor and was continually entertained by the parents. While crawling around, an elderly man, wearing an old floppy hat walks over, slowly maneuvers around the child to a chair close by and sits down. He leisurely bows his head as his floppy hat droops down over his eyes as if taking a nap. The little child sees the elderly man and crawls over towards him. The little one grabs hold of the chair leg, pulls up, and stares at the elderly man. The elderly man calmly lifts up his head and sees the child smiling at him. He smiles back and says, "Well, look at you, - one, two, three, four; you have the same amount of teeth I have."

An arrogant person believes that a child cannot teach them anything. A wise person believes that even a little child can teach them something new. Always be willing to learn something other than what you already know. Believe it or not, that child may one day be your doctor, teacher, or your President.

Something new I recently learned is:

Something that I've learned from children is:

EPILOGUE

Smoke filled the skies of what was carefully created by a whisper in the wind as planes flew into tall buildings, dropping bombs, and missiles glided across land designed for peace. Men, women, and children caring small and heavy artillery invented in order to defend their homes, their families, and their lives from others that wanted to conquer and take control. Millions of lives ended because of a misunderstanding, a few choice words, the color of one's skin, the belief of one's religion, and no one cared enough to ask why. No one cared enough to pray. No one cared enough to think before they acted. And no one noticed the dark mass that was filling the skies, covering, removing the sun from its existence; nor the silence of the birds. No one noticed the trees no longer swaying; but burning into oblivion, or the ocean no longer moving; as the wind blew its last breath.

No one could foresee what happened next. Then there was silence; then there was nothing. Darkness once more filled the universe; then a whisper. Then there was life.

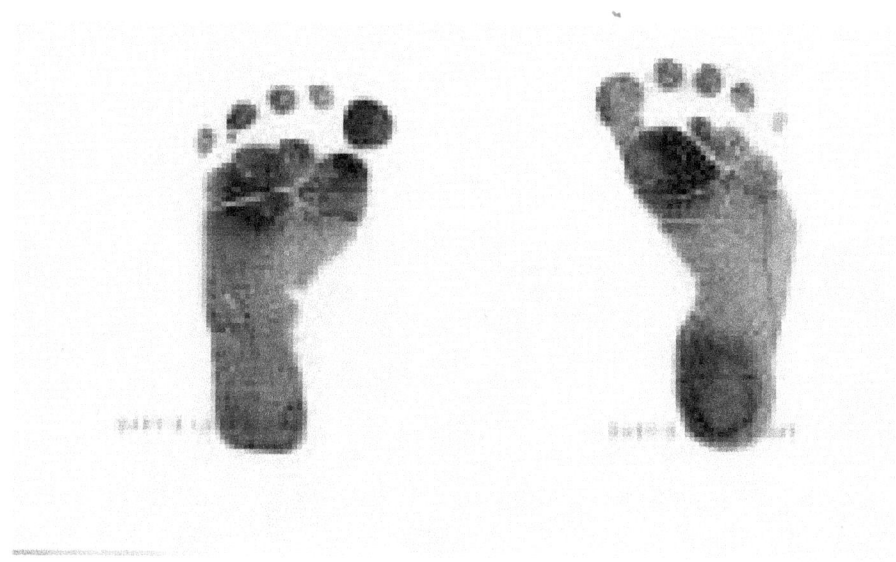

New Beginnings

A new day has begun

As a distant breeze rolls across the fields of dreams

Bringing forth a new beginning; blowing away days before

Leaving traces of what was and what is to become

As a new day has begun

Do we choose our path in life or does the life we lead choose our path?

Are you willing to walk *the path* that takes you to unknown destinations in order to search for the real meaning of the life that you were unwillingly born into because another's hand played a part in your creation so that you could fulfill the task that were specifically designed just for you?

Are you willing to walk that path *of uncertainty* while facing all the obstacles that has been predestined to make you fail so that you could understand without failure, there is no success?

Are you willing to travel the road that *leads to* heartache and pain, while shedding the tears of grief because you feel that you are unable to continue on a road that's filled with hills, valleys, curves, and in your heart you know it's a dead end but something within you will not allow you to quit?

Are you willing to take *a journey* that's filled with unpredictable changes in which you begin to question your very existence?

Are you willing to walk the path *in search of* something greater than yourself regardless of the consequences, disappointments, obstacles, failures, heartaches, ups and downs, the unknowing, and the unpredictable changes that may occur?

If you are willing to walk this path from birth until you have gracefully aged with time and taken the road many have travelled, only few succeed; then you have fulfilled your life's purpose and discovered that you are . . .

the essence of wisdom and life.

Actions that I will take to fulfill my journey:

This is who I am and the current path in life that I am taking:

The journey continues . . . .

Acknowledgements

My "brother" PABLO and COLLYN, thank you for always having a listening ear and the much needed meditation sessions we've shared together. Thank you TRICIA for allowing me to be ME.

Thanks to JUREE SERENE for naming this book before I even thought of writing it.

ADRIANA, INDIA, and KAI – Your life's journey has already been written; you only need to follow the right path in order to reach your destination. As you travel down this path, these things you should know: Listen not with just your ears; but your heart as well. See with not just your eyes; because they can be misleading. Look within a person's heart, their soul, and there you will find the truth. Finally, never stop seeking the WISDOM that LIFE has to offer.

Thank you STEPHANIE, JENNIFER, ERIKA, LESLI, and SHANA for being my second pair of eyes and ears. You always seem to know when I've reached my limit.

Dr. MANN, you have been a confidant, a good listener, and an advisor. Thank you for your continuous support.

Drs. MAUSBACH and CARDENAS, thank you for your support and guidance over the past few years. You have been a mentor and an instrument in my search for The Essence of Wisdom and Life.

Thank you BEVERLY BLACK JOHNSON, RACHEL BERRY, and authors, CHERYL LACEY DONOVAN and KIM ROBINSON for inviting me to "GUMBO for the SOUL" Blog Talk Radio to shed some light on foster children.

About the Author

Dahveed is a freelance writer, the author of the 2005 release - *Through The Eyes of A Foster Child: A Poetic Journey*, his first book of poetry and prose which focuses on foster children. In 2010 he released *Before I Was Born: I Saw The World Through Your Eyes* which is a book of poetry for children and expectant mothers. Dahveed is working on other projects to be released in 2012 and 2013. He currently resides in Southern California.

Also by Dahveed

POETRY

Beyond The Horizon

Black In The Day

Dawn

Let It Flow

Let Our Children Speak

Rainy Days

The Power of Three

The Strength of A Man

The Writer's Block

Turn On and Tune In

Unforgettable Silence

Unity

and other works not listed

ARTICLES and ESSAYS

African American Children in the Foster Care System

B Is For Beating

Building Self Esteem in Foster Children

Child Abuse

Educating Our Foster Children

Independent Living Skills for Foster Children

www.ingramcontent.com/pod-product-compliance
Lightning Source LLC
Chambersburg PA
CBHW081014040426
42444CB00014B/3206